impact

1

Grammar Book

T0349564

Australia · Brazil · Mexico · Singapore · United Kingdom · United States

impact

1

Grammar Book

Present simple

In and *on*

A red fox exploring Bristol, UK

We use the **present simple** to talk about:
- things in general.

*I **live** next to the High Line.*

*It **gets** hot in Spain in the summer.*

- things we do regularly or often.

*The musicians **play** every Saturday.*

*He **visits** his grandparents every weekend.*

- permanent states.

*The High Line **is** in New York City.*

*My mum **lives** in Spain.*

In the third person singular affirmative (*he*, *she*, *it*), we add *-s* to the verb.

grow ⟶ *grows*

visit ⟶ *visits*

We add *-es* to verbs which end in *-ss*, *-sh*, *-ch*, *-x* and *-o* in the third person singular affirmative.

dress ⟶ *dresses*

wash ⟶ *washes*

catch ⟶ *catches*

mix ⟶ *mixes*

go ⟶ *goes*

When a verb ends in a consonant + *-y*, we take off the *-y* and add *-ies* in the third person singular affirmative.

carry ⟶ *carries*

When a verb ends in a vowel + *-y*, we just add *-s* in the third person singular affirmative.

stay ⟶ *stays*

In the negative and question forms, we use the auxiliary verb *do/does* and the main verb in its infinitive form.

*The High Line **doesn't stay** open all night.*

*The residents **don't meet** on Wednesdays.*

***Does** she **like** going to the park?*

***Do** you **think** green spaces are important?*

In short answers, we only use *do/does*. We don't use the main verb.

***Does** she **like** going to the park? No, she **doesn't**.*

***Do** you **think** green spaces are important? Yes, I **do**.*

➔ See grammar box on page 52.

1 **Complete the table.**

Verb	Third person singular	Verb	Third person singular
open	opens	live	
enjoy		worry	
go		explore	
allow		build	
sell		watch	

2 **Circle the correct verb.**

Example: I **go** / **goes** to the park every weekend.

1. The park **protect** / **protects** the animals.
2. London **has** / **have** a lot of green spaces.
3. The park **close** / **closes** at night.
4. We **spend** / **spends** a lot of time outdoors in the summer.
5. The bridge **go** / **goes** over the river.
6. She **pay** / **pays** to go to concerts in the park.
7. People **don't** / **doesn't** have enough information about nature in urban areas.
8. Architects **design** / **designs** buildings.

3 **Complete the sentences with the negative form of the present simple.**

Example: I **don't live** in London. (live)

1. They _____ the museum very often. (visit)
2. She _____ to the park every day. (go)
3. He _____ festivals. (enjoy)
4. The park _____ at night. (close)
5. Children _____ to pay to go to the concert. (need)
6. He _____ at weekends. (work)
7. People _____ next to the river. (walk)
8. She _____ trees. (plant)

In and *on* are prepositions of place. We use them to say where things are located. We use *in* for objects or places within or inside something.

Lion City is in eastern China.
His hands are in his pockets.
There are many archways in Lion City.

We use *on* for objects or places on the surface or on top of something.

Lion City is not on a mountain.
There are sculptures of animals on these archways.
His hands are not on the table.

REMEMBER

Sometimes, *in* and *on* have different meanings when they are attached to specific nouns. The meaning will usually be clear from the context.

For example, *on* the plane/train/bus is more likely to mean *within* the plane/train/bus NOT *on top of* it!
He sat in the chair is more likely to mean *on top of* the chair NOT *within* the chair!

1 **Complete the sentences with *in* or *on*.**

Example: *Shi Cheng is an ancient city in China.*

1. China is _____ Asia.

2. London is _____ the river Thames.

3. There are many sculptures _____ Shi Cheng.

4. There is a butterfly _____ the flower.

5. There are lots of butterflies _____ the garden.

6. Most cities _____ Europe have green spaces.

7. There are lots of cafés _____ the neigbourhood.

8. This is my favourite place _____ Earth.

9. They live _____ an island in the Pacific Ocean.

10. We saw lots of rubbish _____ the sea.

2 (Circle) the correct word.

Example: *He phoned to say he was **in** /(**on**) the train.*

1. There are lots of boats **in** / **on** the river.
2. He went on a discovery walk **in** / **on** the city.
3. There are lots of tall skyscrapers **in** / **on** the capital.
4. He spends too much time **in** / **on** his phone.
5. Look at the posters **in** / **on** the wall.
6. He planted lots of vegetables **in** / **on** the garden.
7. Birds build nests **in** / **on** trees.
8. There's a new shopping centre **in** / **on** my town.
9. There are some amazing videos **in** / **on** the Internet.
10. I like to relax **in** / **on** my home.

3 **Are these sentences correct?** Tick the correct sentences. Rewrite the incorrect sentences.

Example: *She reads the news in TV.*
        *She reads the news **on** TV.*

1. There are lots of rural areas in Kazakhstan.

   _____

2. There are tall skyscrapers on the city.

   _____

3. Have you got a map on your bag?

   _____

4. You can see many green spaces in London.

   _____

5. He took photographs on three different continents.

   _____

6. People like to walk in the High Line paths.

   _____

7. Every weekend we have a picnic in the High Line gardens.

   _____

8. The city is in the coast.

   _____

Present simple questions and answers

Possessives

NASA astronauts working underwater on a Hubble telescope model

We use the **present simple** to talk about things we do:

● regularly or often.

*Does a pastry chef **wear** a uniform?*

*Yes, he **does**./No, he **doesn't**.*

*Do pastry chefs **work** every day?*

*Yes, they **do**./No, they **don't**.*

● as part of a routine.

*How **do** you **create** beautiful desserts?*

*I **plan** the design. Then I **find** the right ingredients.*

In the negative and question forms, we use the auxiliary verb *do/does* and the main verb in its infinitive form.

*The players **don't practise** on Tuesdays.*

*Where **does** a waiter **work**?*

➲ See grammar box on page 52.

REMEMBER

In short answers, we only use *do/does*. We don't use the main verb.

Does she wear a uniform for work?

*No, she **doesn't**.*

Do you love your job?

*Yes, I **do**.*

---

1 **Complete the table.**

Verb	Third person singular	Verb	Third person singular	Verb	Third person singular
drive	drives	try		catch	
bake		cook		wash	
do		hurry		train	
dress		clean		explore	

2 **Complete the sentences with the negative form of the present simple.**

Example: *I **don't wear** a uniform. (wear)*

1. They _____ to work. (drive)

2. She _____ food. (prepare)

3. They _____ for big groups. (cook)

4. The restaurant _____ on Mondays. (open)

5. She _____ Japanese. (speak)

6. He _____ risks in his job. (take)

7. I _____ to work in an office. (want)

8. They _____ during the winter. (train)

3 **Complete the questions with the present simple.** Write the answers.

Example: ***Do you wear** a uniform at work? (you / wear)* ✔ ***Yes, I do.***

1. _____ outside? (the researchers / work) ✔ _____

2. _____ an assistant? (the head chef / have) ✔ _____

3. _____ underwater? (they / train) ✔ _____

4. _____ how to dive? (the students / know) ✘ _____

5. _____ exploring caves? (you / enjoy) ✔ _____

6. _____ lots of skills? (the entertainers / need) ✔ _____

7. _____ lots of time off? (the waiters / get) ✘ _____

8. _____ the food? (the captain / cook) ✘ _____

4 **Use the prompts to write questions in the present simple.**

Example: *where / your brother / work*   ***Where does your brother work?***

1. who / he / work with   _____

2. when / your brother / finish work   _____

3. why / you / ask so many questions   _____

4. what / firefighters / wear to work   _____

5. when / you / start work   _____

6. how often / your boss / work late   _____

7. why / you / not enjoy your job   _____

8. why / you / train as a chef   _____

Possessives: Showing ownership

We show **ownership** in two ways:
• With an **apostrophe** and an **s**:
Singular: **'s**
This dentist's job isn't done in an office.
Plural: **s'**
Pilots' days are very long.
• With a **possessive adjective**:
My job is helping ill people. What's your job?

REMEMBER

The possessive adjective replaces *the* or *a.*
The job is exciting. ⟶ *My job is exciting.*

Subject pronouns	I	you	he/she/it	we	you	they
Possessive adjectives	my	your	his/her/its	our	your	their

① **Complete the sentences with possessive adjectives.**

Example: *My job is in the city. (I)*

1. The ship has _____ own pool. (it)

2. Where is _____ office? (you)

3. _____ journey to work takes an hour. (they)

4. _____ job is very dangerous. (she)

5. Photography is _____ passion. (he)

6. _____ dad is a scientist. (we)

② **Change the sentences using an apostrophe and an s.**

Example: *The friends of my sister.   My sister's friends.*

1. The job of your father.   _____

2. The mother of the orangutan.   _____

3. The teeth of my patients.   _____

4. The skills of their doctors.   _____

5. The goal of the service.   _____

6. The choice of your parents.   _____

3 **Match the sentence halves.**

1. The dentists often visit
2. He's a college professor but
3. My sister is happy with
4. Our train was delayed so
5. I learnt Spanish because
6. Can you tell me if this
7. London is famous

a. her career choice.
b. is your book?
c. their patients in unusual places.
d. I need it for my job.
e. for its architecture.
f. his job is to explore underwater.
g. we missed the opening.

4 **Are these sentences correct?** Tick the correct sentences. Rewrite the incorrect sentences.

Example: *The dentists chair is very comfortable.*
          The dentist's chair is very comfortable.

1. My parent's friend is an explorer.

_____

2. Dr Jones's job is to collect rock samples.

_____

3. Jimmys' job is exciting.

_____

4. Mr and Mrs Evans both love his jobs.

_____

5. My dads goals are to be happy and healthy.

_____

6. The childrens' aunt is in Alaska.

_____

7. Will scientists discover ice on Jupiter's moons?

_____

8. Dangerous jobs have our advantages.

_____

WRITING

Write an interview about a family member's job. Use present simple questions and possessives.

Example: *What **does** your father like about **his** job?*
          *My father flies planes. He loves **his** job because pilots' roles are so varied. **Their** routes change every day.*

Present continuous

At, *on* and *in*

Blue ghost fireflies

We use the **present continuous** to talk about:
- things that are in progress at the time of speaking.

*What **are** they **doing**? They're **eating** their lunch.*
- things that are in progress around the time of speaking or that are temporary.

*He's **looking** for a new flat.*

The present continuous is formed with *am/are/is* and the main verb with the *-ing* ending.

jump ⟶ *jumping*

When the verb ends in -e, we take off the -e and add *-ing*.

make ⟶ *making*

When the verb ends in a vowel + consonant, we double the final consonant and add *-ing*.

win ⟶ *winning*

When the verb ends in *-l*, we double the *-l* and add *-ing*.

cancel ⟶ *cancelling*

When the verb ends in -ie, we take off the -ie and add -y and -ing.

tie ⟶ *tying*
lie ⟶ *lying*
die ⟶ *dying*

We can use time expressions such as *now, at the moment, these days, at present, today,* etc., with the present continuous.

*She's washing her car **at the moment**.*

➔ See grammar box on page 52.

1 **Write the *-ing* form of the verbs in the box in the correct column of the table.**

| worry   live   come   hunt   hide   hit   give   look   hide |
| put   write   run   sit   stop   study   swim   sleep   read |

get ⟶ getting	ride ⟶ riding	play ⟶ playing
		worrying

2 **Complete the sentences with the affirmative form of the present continuous.**

Example: *I'm working in England. (work)*

1. They _____ in Spain. (live)

2. The sun _____. (set)

3. Look! That plant _____. (grow)

4. The baby monkeys _____. (sleep)

5. We _____ about time zones. (learn)

6. I _____ to understand the problem. (try)

7. We _____ the film about whales. (enjoy)

8. My sister _____ a year in Italy. (spend)

3 **Complete the sentences with the negative form of the present continuous.**

Example: *I'm not wearing a coat today. (wear)*

1. They _____ to work because there is too much traffic. (drive)

2. She _____ to the cinema tonight. (go)

3. The owls _____ right now. (hunt)

4. The cubs _____ with each other. (playing)

5. I _____ this film. (enjoy)

6. He _____ any more. (train)

7. They _____ for the location today. (search)

8. My friends _____ to New York. (fly)

4 **Complete the questions with the present continuous.** Write the answers.

Example: *Are you working on the ship? (you / work)* ✔ *Yes, I am.*

1. _____ suitable clothes? (they / wear)   ✗ _____

2. _____ by bus? (you / travel)   ✔ _____

3. _____ a good time? (you / have)   ✔ _____

4. _____ in the city? (your parents / live)   ✗ _____

5. _____ right now? (we / leave)   ✔ _____

6. _____ outside? (it / rain)   ✗ _____

7. _____ to me? (he / talk)   ✔ _____

8. _____ dark? (it / get)   ✔ _____

At, on and *in*: Saying when things happen

At, *on* and *in* are prepositions of time. We use them to say when things happen.

We use *on* with days and dates.
on Monday(s) / **on** my birthday / **on** New Year's Day / **on** 1ˢᵗ June

We use *in* with months, years, seasons and times of day.
in May / **in** 2017 / **in** winter / **in** the holidays / **in** the morning

We usually use *at* with exact times and certain expressions.
at eight o'clock / **at** night / **at** the weekend / **at** Christmas

1 **Write the time expressions in the correct column of the table.**

| New Year's Day   August   Mondays   1066   the 1990s   9 p.m. |
| Sunday morning   quarter to twelve   midday   1ˢᵗ January   Midsummer's Day |
| the early morning   winter   the end of the day   eleven o'clock |

at	on	in
	New Year's Day	

2 **Circle the correct word.**

Example: *at /* **on** *Tuesdays*

1. **in** / **on** Tuesday morning

2. **in** / **on** the early morning of Tuesday

3. **at** / **on** the end of Tuesday

4. **at** / **on** the first Tuesday **in** / **on** August

5. **at** / **on** the end of the day **at** / **on** Tuesday

6. one Tuesday morning **in** / **on** the early 1980s

3 Complete the sentences with *at*, *on* or *in*.

We went to Morocco _____in_____ December. [1]_____ summer it is too hot in Morocco, but [2]_____ winter, the temperature is perfect. [3]_____ Wednesday, after two days in Marrakesh, we went down to the coast at Essaouira. [4]_____ the evening of the first day, we went for a walk around the city. [5]_____ sunset, we went to a lovely restaurant. [6]_____ Thursday morning we went to the beach, where my sister and I tried kite-surfing and my parents went horse-riding. [7]_____ lunchtime, we went to the old fishing port. Finally, [8]_____ the afternoon, we visited the traditional market, where I bought a beautiful blanket. It was an amazing trip.

4 Complete the email with *at*, *on* or *in*.

Subject: Hello from the Arctic

Hi Anna,

Thanks for your email. Of course I can tell you about my town! I live in the Arctic, in a place called Tromsø. _____In_____ winter, it hardly gets light. There are 20 hours of darkness every day. However, [1]_____ summer, the sun doesn't set and there is daylight [2]_____ midnight! There is so much to do here. You can go on a whale safari [3]_____ eleven o'clock [4]_____ night, or go swimming in the sea [5]_____ three o'clock [6]_____ the morning! You can't do that [7]_____ January, though, because it's far too cold. My birthday is [8]_____ 22nd January, and we always go to North Cape to have dinner and see the northern lights. They're amazing! Can you see them from your city?

Write soon!

Brigitte

WRITING

Write a holiday postcard to a friend, using the present continuous and *at*, *on* or *in*.

Example: ***I am writing*** this from France. ***We are enjoying*** our holiday. ***On*** Monday we went to the beach in Biarritz ***in*** the morning.

Modals

A rhinoceros and its caretaker at a conservancy in Kenya

Modal verbs are verbs which do not function on their own. They require a second verb, in the form of a bare infinitive.

We use **must** and **have to**:
• to talk about obligation and necessity.
*We **must** save rhinos.*
*They **have to** do something about poaching.*
• to talk about the present and the future.
*We **must** stop killing rhinos now.*
*We **have to** visit the rhino sanctuary next year.*

We use **mustn't** to talk about things we are not allowed to do (prohibition).
*I **mustn't** be late.*

We use **don't have to** to talk about what is not necessary or obligatory.
*We **don't have to** use rhino horn products.*

We use **should** and **shouldn't** for recommendations and suggestions.
*You **should** run a marathon to raise money.*
*We **shouldn't** ignore the problem.*

➜ See grammar box on page 52.

1 **Complete the sentences with *must* or *mustn't*.**

Example: *We **mustn't** kill endangered species.* ✗

1. You _____ use rhino horn products. ✗

2. Elephants _____ be protected. ✔

3. We _____ dig up sea turtle eggs. ✗

4. Rangers _____ protect the parks. ✔

5. You _____ buy ivory. ✗

6. They _____ frighten the baboons away. ✔

7. We _____ destroy animals' habitats. ✗

8. We _____ look after the environment. ✔

2 **Is the idea *necessary* (N) or *recommended* (R)?** Write N or R.

Example: *We should clean up the beaches.*   __R__

1. You mustn't throw litter in nature reserves.   _____

2. You shouldn't use so much plastic.   _____

3. We must try to avoid human-wildlife conflict.   _____

4. You mustn't light fires in the national park.   _____

5. You must not leave your vehicle.   _____

6. They shouldn't drive so close to the elephants!   _____

7. You shouldn't be afraid of rats.   _____

8. You must leave the park by sunset.   _____

3 **Complete the sentences with *must, have/has to* or *should/shouldn't* according to the clues given in brackets.**

Example: *You **should** listen to his advice. (a good idea)*

1. You _____ stay behind the fence. (necessary)

2. He _____ learn about the animals' behaviour. (necessary)

3. She _____ take the injured turtle to the hospital. (a good idea)

4. We _____ tell people about the problem. (a good idea)

5. We _____ stop people taking the eggs. (necessary)

6. I _____ train for four years. (necessary)

7. Bears _____ live in their natural habitat. (a good idea)

8. They _____ go back to the forest now. (necessary)

4 **Circle the correct word.**

Example: *You **shouldn't** / **don't have to** ignore the problem.*

1. You **mustn't / don't have to** drive quickly in the reserve.

2. She **doesn't have to / don't have to** take another exam this year.

3. We **must / mustn't** mistreat animals.

4. We **don't have to / shouldn't** destroy their habitat.

5. The villagers **have to / has to** wear masks.

6. We **should / shouldn't** take the turtle's eggs.

7. We **must / don't have to** use rhino horn for medicine.

8. People **don't have to / doesn't have to** have monitors in their homes.

We use **can** and **can't**:
- to talk about ability in the present.

*Elephants **can** communicate over long distances.*
*They **can't** climb trees.*

We use **could** and **couldn't**:
- to talk about ability in the past.

*People thought of ways they **could** help the crabs.*
*Before 2011, elephants **couldn't** safely cross a road in Kenya.*

➔ See grammar box on page 52.

1 **Complete the sentences with *can* or *can't* and the verb in brackets.**

Example: *Tunnels under roads **can help** elephants. (help)*

1. _____ we _____ more species with this project? (help)

2. Animals _____ without water. (not survive)

3. Scientists _____ computers to check on animals in the forest. (use)

4. Wildlife bridges _____ animal lives. (save)

5. The crabs _____ the road safely. (not cross)

6. Elephants _____ over long distances. (communicate)

7. We _____ why the animals are dying. (not understand)

8. We _____ anything about it. (not do)

9. How _____ we _____ the Antiguan racer snake? (save)

10. They _____ enough food. (not find)

2 **Match the questions to the answers.**

1. Could elephants in Kenya cross roads safely before 2011?

2. Can they understand how to avoid traffic?

3. Could the tunnel help preserve wildlife?

4. Can the snake kill you?

5. Could they rescue the injured bird?

a. Yes, it could.

b. Yes, they could.

c. No, they couldn't.

d. Yes, they can now.

e. Yes, it can.

3 **Use the prompts to write questions and answers.**

Example: *you / help me? (present)*
> **Can you help me?** ✔ *Yes, I can.*

1. bear cubs / survive on their own? (present)

_____ ✗ _____

2. elephants / cross roads safely? (past)

_____ ✗ _____

3. we / help? (present)

_____ ✔ _____

4. you / make a poster for the campaign? (present)

_____ ✔ _____

5. the turtles / lay their eggs safely? (past)

_____ ✗ _____

6. crabs / avoid cars? (past)

_____ ✗ _____

7. the poachers / be caught? (present)

_____ ✔ _____

8. I / do more to help? (present)

_____ ✔ _____

4 **Circle the correct word.**

Example: *I looked, but I **can't** / **couldn't** find the article on the Internet.*

1. The divers thought they **can** / **could** see the whale.
2. They **can't** / **couldn't** see the snake because it was well hidden.
3. Nowadays, people **can** / **could** communicate with each other very easily.
4. We **can't** / **couldn't** fly to Iceland last week because of the volcano.
5. Fifty years ago, scientists **can't** / **couldn't** use data tracking devices.
6. The new equipment means that we **can** / **could** go deeper than ever before.

WRITING

Write:

1. a list of five rules or recommendations for preserving the environment, and
2. five things you can do yourself.

Example: *I **must** use less plastic* ⟶ *I **can** take my own bag to the supermarket.*

Past simple

A man in a protective suit, ready to explore the Darvaza Crater, Turkmenistan

We use the **past simple** to talk about:
- things in the past which have finished.
*I **travelled** to Greece last year.*
- things in the past which were habits.
*I **walked** on the beach every morning.*
- things in the past that were true.
*Women in Ancient Greece **liked** long hair and **used** olive oil to make it shine.*

We form the past simple affirmative of regular verbs by adding the -ed ending.

work ——→ *worked*

When the verb ends in -e, we add -d.

believe ——→ *believed*

When the verb ends in a consonant and -y, we take off the -y and add -ied.

carry ——→ *carried*

In the negative and question forms, we use the auxiliary verb *did/didn't* and the main verb in its infinitive form.
*Ancient Greek men **didn't like** short hair.*
***Did** they **wear** trousers?*
*What **did** they **wear** on their feet?*

In short answers, we only use *did/didn't*. We don't use the main verb.
***Did** they wear sandals? Yes, they **did**./No, they **didn't**.*

➔ See grammar box on page 53.

---

1 **Complete the sentences.** Use the verbs in the box in the past simple.

change	clean	dress up	like	replace	show	~~study~~	wash

Example: *My sister **studied** fashion at university.*

1. I cut up my old jeans and _____ them from trousers into shorts.

2. Yesterday, I _____ all the dirty clothes.

3. I grew out of my old uniform so we _____ it with a bigger one.

4. Dad _____ our shoes with polish to make them shiny.

5. I really _____ my old school uniform because it was very comfortable and practical.

6. My little brother _____ as a pirate for his friend's birthday party.

7. I _____ my mum the trainers in the shop but she said they were too expensive.

2 **Complete the sentences with the negative form of the past simple.**

Example: Julia **didn't pierce** her ears until she was 16. (pierce)

1. People in the 18th century _____ jeans. (wear)

2. In the past, firefighters _____ protective clothing. (have)

3. I _____ the accessories you gave me. (use)

4. Mrs Peters _____ her necklace. (sell)

5. I _____ comfortable in the grey suit. (feel)

6. The students agreed that they _____ the look of the new uniform. (like)

7. Davis and Strauss _____ denim trousers until 1873. (make)

8. I _____ to dress up to go to the party. (want)

3 **Use the prompts to write questions in the past simple.**

Example: how / Ancient Greeks / wear their hair
        How did Ancient Greeks wear their hair?

1. Ancient Greeks / like dark hair   _____

2. what / Ancient Greeks / use to colour their hair   _____

3. why / Ancient Greek women / use oil in their hair _____

4. what / lots of jewellery / mean in ancient China   _____

5. what / Ndebele men / offer their wives   _____

6. when / Ndebele women / remove their rings   _____

7. where / Indian women / paint henna   _____

8. what / Maori men / do to their faces   _____

4 **Write answers to the questions in Activity 3.** Look up the answers in your Student's Book if necessary.

Example: How did Ancient Greeks wear their hair?
        They wore their hair long.

1. _____

2. _____

3. _____

4. _____

5. _____

6. _____

7. _____

8. _____

Past simple: Saying what happened

Many important verbs are irregular, which means that they do not follow the same pattern as regular verbs. We do not add *-ed* to make the past simple. These verbs don't change form in the past simple. *I (she/he/it/we/you/they)* **put** *on red glasses.*

➔ See the irregular verbs list on page 55.

1 **Complete the table with the past simple of these verbs.**

Verb	Past simple	Verb	Past simple	Verb	Past simple
begin	*began*	go		give	
think		bring		get	
keep		have		take	

2 **Change the sentences into the past simple.**

Example: *Footballers wear their own clothes.*
Footballers wore their own clothes.

1. Mrs Riley teaches English.

   _____

2. I take my scarf to every match.

   _____

3. I go clothes shopping in the market.

   _____

4. My grandmother keeps her jewellery in a locked box.

   _____

5. My employers give me a new uniform.

   _____

6. My white trainers get dirty very quickly.

   _____

7. I have seven pairs of denim jeans.

   _____

8. I often buy clothes online.

   _____

3 Match the questions to the answers.

1. What did Anna wear to work?
2. What did you buy in Italy?
3. What did you draw in your art class?
4. Why did doctors put on special suits?
5. What did you think of the fashions?
6. What did you make in your spare time?
7. Did you take an umbrella with you?
8. Did the uniform keep the players cool?

a. I bought new sunglasses and a hat.
b. They put them on to protect themselves.
c. I made jewellery and accessories.
d. No, I forgot to pack it.
e. She wore a suit, tights and high heels.
f. Yes, it did.
g. I thought they were very practical.
h. I drew pictures of designer clothes.

4 Are these sentences correct? Tick the correct sentences. Rewrite the incorrect sentences.

Example: *I goed to Italy last year.*
            *I **went** to Italy last year.*

1. It was hot, so I weared shorts every day.

_____

2. I studied fashion at college.

_____

3. We buyed a lot of clothes at the shopping centre.

_____

4. I visited The Costume Institute in New York.

_____

5. My grandma maked me a jumper for my birthday.

_____

6. We had a great time at the show.

_____

7. We all thinked Italy was amazing!

_____

8. We taked home lots of souvenirs.

_____

WRITING

Write a description of what people wore in the past, using both regular and irregular past simple verbs, comparing it to what they wear now.

Example: *Some men **wore** tights in the past, but now only women **wear** tights.*

Adjectives

Countable and uncountable nouns

Sea is for Cookie, a mash-up created from *The Great Wave off Kanagawa* and a television character called Cookie Monster

We use the comparative form to compare two people, animals or things. We often use the word *than* after the comparative form.

*She's **faster than** me.*

*This new sport is **more interesting than** basketball.*

We can use two comparative statements one after the other to compare more than two things.

*Cricket is a **faster** sport **than** bowls, but it is **slower than** football.*

To make the comparative form of adjectives with one syllable, we add the ending *-er*.

fast ⟶ *faster*

When the adjective ends in:

• -e, add *-r*.

close ⟶ *closer*

• -y, take off the -y and add *-ier*.

early ⟶ *earlier*

• a vowel + consonant, double the last consonant and add *-er*.

big ⟶ *bigger*

We use the word *more* with some two-syllable and with three-syllable (and longer) adjectives.

interesting ⟶ *more interesting*

Some two-syllable adjectives have two comparative forms.

simple ⟶ *simpler/more simple*

clever ⟶ *cleverer/more clever*

Some adjectives are irregular and do not follow these rules.

good ⟶ *better*

bad ⟶ *worse*

We also use *less* and *as ... as* to make comparative statements.

*Basketball is **less exciting than** rugby.*

*Football is **as fun as** hockey.*

---

1 **Write the comparative form of each word.**

1. active _____

2. strong _____

3. popular _____

4. frightening _____

5. easy _____

6. difficult _____

7. traditional _____

8. healthy _____

9. boring _____

10. delicious _____

11. weird _____

12. cool _____

2 Complete the sentences with the comparative form.

Example: *Baseball is* **more difficult than** *cricket. (+/difficult)*

1. Baseball is _____ cricket. (+/easy)

2. I think they are _____ each other. (=/hard)

3. She's _____ me at football. (+/good)

4. Rugby is _____ I expected. (-/fun)

5. I got _____ I have ever been. (+/exhausted)

6. Indoor cricket is a _____ game _____ one-day cricket. (+/quick)

7. Bossaball is a _____ game _____ basketball. (+/fun)

8. I am _____ my brother. (+/active)

3 **Read the sentences.** Combine them to make two different comparative statements using the adjective in brackets.

Example: *Football is fast. Basketball is faster.*
Football is **slower than** *basketball. (slow)*
Basketball is **quicker than** *football. (quick)*

1. Fishing is boring. Walking is enjoyable.

   a. Fishing is _____ (exciting)

   b. Walking is _____ (fun)

2. Volcano boarding is crazy! Sandboarding is boring.

   a. Volcano boarding is _____ (crazy)

   b. Sandboarding is _____ (crazy)

3. Rugby is a violent sport. Bowls isn't a violent sport.

   a. Bowls isn't _____ (violent)

   b. Rugby is _____ (violent)

WRITING

Write the script of a discussion between two friends, using comparative statements.

Example: *A: I think reading is* **more enjoyable than** *sport.*
B: No way! I love sport. Playing football is **more exciting than** *reading about it.*
A: Sure, but in general, using your imagination when reading is **more exciting than** *any sport.*

Nouns that we can count (i.e. nouns that we can use in the plural) are called **countable nouns**. When the subject of a sentence is in the plural, the verb must also be in the plural. We use *a few/many* with countable nouns.

Countable nouns
A few / Some / A lot of / Many meals **are** a mix of food from different cultures.
How many chefs **combine** foods from different cultures?
Two / A few / Some / A lot of / Many chefs **combine** foods from different cultures.
*Restaurants usually have **a couple of / three / too many** special dishes.*

Nouns that we cannot count and that do not have plurals are called **uncountable nouns**. We do not use **a/an** with uncountable nouns. We use *a little/much* with uncountable nouns. When the subject of a sentence is an uncountable noun, the verb must be in the singular form.

Uncountable nouns
A little / Some / A lot of / Much fruit **is** used in food from different cultures.
How much cheese **is** on a Japanese-Italian pizza?
There **is a little / some / a lot of** cheese.
*Dessert sushi sometimes **has a piece of /some / too much** fruit in it.*

1 **Complete the sentences with the correct word or phrase.**

Example: *There is **a lot of** food on the table. (a lot of / many)*

1. _____ of the food is savoury. (Some / A few)

2. There are also _____ sweet dishes. (many / much)

3. Would you like to try _____ cake? (a few / some)

4. No, thank you. I have already eaten _____ sandwiches. (much / a lot of)

5. Would you like _____ tea, then? (a few / a little)

6. Yes, please, I would love _____. (some / many)

7. There are _____ different spices in this dish. (a few / a little)

8. I only used _____ chilli because I know you don't like spicy food. (a little / much)

2 (Circle) the correct word.

Example: *In Spain, there are* **much** / **many** *different types of food.*

Throughout the country, they use [1] **many** / **a lot of** olive oil in their cooking. In the north, however, they use [2] **a few** / **a little** more butter.

Spanish fishermen provide [3] **much** / **a couple of** the country's fish, but Spain also imports [4] **a little** / **some** of its fish from around the world. There are [5] **a little** / **a lot of** fish restaurants on the Atlantic and Mediterranean coasts.

In the countryside, people eat [6] **a few** / **much** more meat than on the coast. When you go to a Spanish restaurant, you can choose from [7] **a lot of** / **much** different dishes called 'tapas'. You can try [8] **many** / **much** different flavours when you eat tapas.

3 **Are these sentences correct?** Tick the correct sentences. Rewrite the incorrect sentences.

Example: *There are much different cuisines in big cities.*
*There are **many** different cuisines in big cities.*

1. How many rice do you want?

   _____

2. The meal was delicious, but there was too many food.

   _____

3. In Mexico, a lot of dishes contain chillies.

   _____

4. Mexican cooking uses a little ingredients.

   _____

5. Much chefs took part in the competition.

   _____

6. Can we add a few more butter to the pan?

   _____

7. Look! There's a small piece of plastic in my food.

   _____

8. I didn't eat many soup at lunchtime.

   _____

WRITING

Write sentences comparing two different sports or types of food. Use countable and uncountable expressions to explain your ideas.

Example: *Cricket is **harder** to understand than football because there are **many** more rules.*

Superlatives

Will and *going to*

A rider using special LED lights on his bicycle wheels for safety, Hong Kong

We use the **superlative** form to compare and rank three or more people, animals or things.

*This is **the scariest** game of all.*

To make the superlative form of adjectives with one syllable, we add the ending -est. We use the word *the* before the adjective.

green ⟶ the greenest

When the adjective ends in:

- -e, add -st.

late ⟶ the latest

- -y, take off the -y and add -iest.

happy ⟶ the happiest

- a vowel + consonant, double the last consonant and add -est.

big ⟶ the biggest

We use the word *most* with adjectives that have two or more syllables to make the superlative form.

famous ⟶ the most famous

We use the word *least* with adjectives to rank people, animals or things in the lowest position.

the least fun, the least difficult

Some adjectives are irregular and do not follow these rules.

good/bad ⟶ the best/the worst

1 **Complete the sentences with the superlative form.**

Example: *Music games are **the most popular** games online (+/popular).*

1. Platform games are _____ and _____. (+/old)(+/good)

2. I think gaming apps are _____ to access. (+/easy)

3. I think gaming is _____ thing you can do on a smartphone. (-/interesting)

4. This puzzle app is _____ app on my smartphone. (+/new)

5. I prefer making films. Some apps have _____ editing software. (+/cool)

6. I installed _____ voice recorder on my tablet. (-/expensive)

7. It's on _____ setting on my smart phone, but it's still very quiet. (+/loud)

8. What are _____ websites you know? (+/funny)

9. My smartphone has _____ battery – that's why I chose it! (+/powerful)

10. That free download app is _____ I have ever tried. (-/bad)

2 Complete the sentences with the superlative form of the adjective.

Example: *Gaming is good. Taking photos is better. Making films is **the best***.

1. My computer is powerful. My sister's is more powerful. Dad's is _____.

2. Your screen is big. Mine is bigger. Mr Rochas' is _____.

3. The homework app is boring. The gaming app is less boring. The football app is _____.

4. My singing app is cool. Yours is cooler. The PopStars one is _____.

5. My battery lasts a long time. My dad's lasts longer, but John's lasts _____.

6. My keyboard is old. My mum's is older. The ones at school are _____.

7. Your tablet is cheap. My tablet is cheaper. This one here is _____.

8. This game is scary. That one is scarier, but the one I saw yesterday was _____.

3 Complete the sentences with a superlative.

Example: *That film is scary. It's **the scariest** film I have ever seen.*

1. My friend George is very clever. He's _____ boy in the class.

2. I love football! It's _____ sport in the world.

3. This game is loud! It's _____ I have ever played!

4. Making movies is fun. It's _____ free-time activity.

5. My friend Camilla is very clever. She's _____ person I know.

6. Alana wears cool clothes. She's probably _____ friend I've got.

7. This camera is really bad. It's _____ I've used.

8. This test is hard! It's _____ test we've taken.

4 Match the sentence halves.

1. French is a difficult language to learn,   a. That's the dirtiest keyboard I've ever seen.

2. The least creative person   b. but Chinese is harder.

3. You should clean your desk!   c. it's the fastest way to travel.

4. My sister can't sing very well.   d. can still have fun with this drawing app.

5. I find maths very difficult,   e. are the clearest pictures I've seen.

6. We went by bullet train because   f. but physics is the hardest subject.

7. The images in this game   g. the least useful app I've got.

8. The Intake App is   h. In fact, I think she's the worst singer I've heard.

When we are talking about the future, we can use:
- *will* (the **future simple**) for things which are possible.
*We **will have** little machines in our heads that can connect to gadgets.*
*People **won't talk** to each other on smartphones anymore.*
***Will** people **need** to have so many gadgets?*
*No, they **won't**. One gadget **will be** all you need.*
- *be going to* for things which are most likely.
*Everything at home **is going to connect** to a gadget.*
*People **aren't going to use** phones with keyboards anymore.*
*How are our gadgets **going to help** us every day?*
*They're **going to help** us do chores, like watering the garden.*

➔ See grammar box on page 53.

1 **Complete the sentences with *will* and the verb in brackets.**

Example: *The Internet **will control** us all! (control)*

1. I know! I _____ this app to translate the text. (use)

2. David _____ us at the technology fair. (meet)

3. In future, I _____ a robot to do all my homework! (get)

4. Radha _____ the information online. (look up)

5. He _____ his research with us yet. (not share)

6. I wonder if robots _____ teachers. (replace)

7. Smartphones _____ smarter than us! (become)

8. Life _____ very different in future. (be)

2 **Match the sentence halves.**

1. When you're eighteen,
2. Are you going to watch
3. Do you think robots will
4. I am going to look for
5. Will Mr Ahmed be
6. They are going to

a. some information about it tonight.
b. will you still live at home?
c. at the meeting tomorrow?
d. spend some time at the museum later.
e. a film at the cinema next weekend?
f. take jobs away from humans?

3 **Complete the sentences with *be going to* and the verb in brackets.**

Example: *We **are going to need** fewer gadgets in future. (need)*

1. I _____ more data next month. (use)

2. The internet _____ more personalised. (become)

3. Companies _____ a lot of information about us. (know)

4. They _____ to Wi-Fi. (not connect)

5. I _____ a day off the internet every week. (have)

6. My brother says he _____ his passwords every week. (not change)

7. I _____ all my homework online. (do)

8. Gaming _____ even faster. (get)

4 **Read the sentences. Tick the best option.**

Example: ☐ *a. I am going to see you tomorrow.*
✔ *b. I will see you tomorrow.*

1. ☐ a. We are going to travel to Mars soon.
   ☐ b. We will travel to Mars soon.

2. ☐ a. Will you visit your friends when you are in Paris?
   ☐ b. Are you going to visit your friends when you are in Paris?

3. ☐ a. Keyboards will disappear and we will dictate everything.
   ☐ b. Keyboards are going to disappear and we are going to dictate everything.

4. ☐ a. Robot chefs are going to work in restaurants.
   ☐ b. Robot chefs will work in restaurants.

5. ☐ a. We won't have to go to shops.
   ☐ b. We aren't going to have to go to shops.

6. ☐ a. I am going to go to school tomorrow.
   ☐ b. I will go to school tomorrow.

7. ☐ a. Everyone will be connected to the internet soon.
   ☐ b. Everyone is going to be connected to the internet soon.

8. ☐ a. Gadgets are going to be part of everyone's life.
   ☐ b. Gadgets will be part of everyone's life.

WRITING

Write a paragraph describing future schools. Use both *will* and *going to*. (Remember: think about whether your prediction is possible or most likely?)

Example: *There **will** be robot teachers in every classroom. However, it **will** be after I leave school so I **am not going to see** it.*

Present perfect

There + to be

In the Hoyo Negro cenote in Mexico, divers Alberto Nava Blank and Susan Bird find the skull of Naia, a teenage girl who lived approximately 13,000 years ago.

Present perfect: Describing a past action that still continues

We use the **present perfect** to talk about:
- things that happened in the past, when we don't say when they happened. Sometimes we use the word *already*. We often use the present perfect to talk about our experiences.

*I **have already eaten**.*

*I **have visited** lots of countries.*
- things which finished a short time ago. We often use the word *just*.

*The teacher **has just left** the room.*

*I **have just been** online.*
- things that still continue into the present. We often use the word *for*.

*They **have played** mancala **for** thousands of years.*

*How long **have** you **used** a computer **for**?*

The present perfect of regular verbs is formed with the auxiliary verb **have/has** and the past participle of the main verb. We put the word **not** after the word **have/has** to make the negative form.

*I **have not played** chess before.*

We put the auxiliary verb **have/has** before the subject to make the question form.

***Have** you **played** chess?*

➡ See grammar box on page 54.

REMEMBER

We form the past participle of irregular verbs in different ways.

do ⟶ did ⟶ done

➡ See irregular verbs list on page 55.

---

1 **Complete the table with irregular past participles.**

Verb	Past simple	Past participle	Verb	Past simple	Past participle
be	was/were	*been*	go	went	
do	did		make	made	
draw	drew		speak	spoke	
say	said		take	took	
drink	drank		write	wrote	
eat	ate		know	knew	

2 **Complete the sentences with the present perfect.**

Example: I **have played** chess since I was five. (play)

1. Archaeologists _____ ancient bones and skulls. (discover)

2. They _____ him any advice. (not give)

3. He _____ his chess piece yet. (not move)

4. They _____ to see the display again. (go back)

5. _____ he _____ many history books? (read)

6. They _____ him for over ten years. (know)

7. I'm going to play a video game because I _____ all my homework. (finish)

8. My parents _____ my brother to the Science Museum. (take)

3 **Complete the questions with the present perfect.** Write the answers.

Example: **Have you tried** squid? (you / try)
     ✔ **Yes, I have.**

1. _____ the game? (they / finish)
  ✗ _____

2. _____ learning about the past? (she / enjoy)
  ✔ _____

3. _____ chess against a computer? (you / play)
  ✔ _____

4. _____ ever _____ of Ötzi? (he / heard)
  ✗ _____

5. _____ ever _____ a mummy? (you / see)
  ✗ _____

6. _____ mancala? (your brother / play)
  ✗ _____

7. _____ ever _____ to Africa? (you / be)
  ✔ _____

8. _____ the game? (we / win)
  ✗ _____

WRITING

Write five sentences saying what you *have* and *haven't done*.

Example: I **have played** the piano for five years but I **have never tried** the violin.

We use **there + to be** in different tenses to express existence and describe the world around us as it *is*, *was*, *has been*, *is going to be* and *will be*.

Present simple
*Now **there's** a Festival of the Sun every year.*
***There are** a lot of different foods to try.*

Past simple
*However, **there wasn't** a Festival of the Sun in Peru between 1535 and 1944.*
***There weren't** any other traditional Incan festivals at that time either.*

Present perfect
***There have** always **been** sun celebrations around the world.*
***There has been** a Festival of the Sun in Peru for centuries.*

Be going to
***Are there going to be** traditional musicians?*
*Yes, **there are going to be** dancers, too.*

Future simple
***Will there be** a lot of people?*
*I think **there will (be)**. It's very popular.*

➔ See grammar box on page 54.

1 **Circle** the correct option.

Example: ***There is*** / ~~**There are**~~ *many festivals in Peru.*

1. **There is / There are** a music festival every year.

2. **There will be / There have been** parades next year.

3. **There is / There are** firework displays in many cities.

4. Last year, **there was / there have been** a record number of visitors to Peru.

5. **There is going to be / There are going to be** even more visitors next year.

6. **There was / There were** more than five hundred people in the ceremony.

7. **There has been / There was** a festival every year since 1978.

8. **There will be / There are** many visitors next year.

2 **Answer the questions.**

Example: *Were there many visitors to Stonehenge last year?* ✔ ***Yes, there were.***

1. Was there a big solstice celebration there? ✔ _____

2. Were there people on top of the stones? ✘ _____

3. Is there usually a barrier around the monument? ✔ _____

4. Has there been a solstice celebration every year? ✘ _____

5. Will there be many people there next year? ✔ _____

6. Is there going to be a change to the time? ✘ _____

7. Was there a time in the past when you could climb on the stones? ✔ _____

8. Were there rules to stop the stones started getting damaged? ✔ _____

3 **Write four pairs of sentences about change in your country.** Use at least two tenses in each pair.

Example: ***There has been*** *a change in attitudes to the environment.* ***There is*** *now a lot more recycling.*

1. _____

_____

2. _____

_____

3. _____

_____

4. _____

_____

WRITING

Write a paragraph about events you have been preparing or practising for. Use the present perfect and *there + to be.*

Example: ***There will be*** *a concert in school next week. I* ***have played*** *my violin every day after school.* ***There were*** *a lot of rehearsals last week.*

Grammar boxes

Units 1 and 2 Present simple

	Affirmative	Negative	Question	Short answers
I / You / We / They	live	don't (do not) live	Do ... live?	Yes, ... do. No, ... don't.
He / She / It	lives	doesn't (does not) live	Do ... live?	Yes, ... does. No, ... doesn't.

Unit 3 Present continuous

	Affirmative	Negative	Question	Short answers
I	'm (am) reading	'm not (am not) reading	Am I reading?	Yes, I am. No, I'm not.
He / She / It	's (is) reading	isn't (is not) reading	Is ... reading?	Yes, ... is. No, ... isn't.
You / We / They	're (are) reading	aren't (are not) reading	Are ... reading?	Yes, ... are. No, ... aren't.

Unit 4 Modals

	Affirmative	Negative	Question	Short answers
I / You / We / They	have to should can must could	don't (do not) have to shouldn't (should not) can't (cannot) mustn't (must not) couldn't (could not)	Do/Don't ... have to ...? Should/Shouldn't ...? Can/Can't ...? Must/Mustn't ...? Could/Couldn't ...?	Yes, ... have to/ should/can/must/ could. No, ... don't have to/ shouldn't/can't/ mustn't/couldn't.
He / She / It	has to	doesn't (does not) have to	Does/Doesn't ... have to ...?	Yes, ... has to. No, ... doesn't have to.

Unit 5 Past simple

	Affirmative	**Negative**	**Question**	**Short answers**
I / You / He / She / It / We / They	liked	didn't (did not) like	Did … like?	Yes, … did. No, … didn't.

Unit 7 Future simple: *Will*

	Affirmative	**Negative**	**Question**	**Short answers**
I / He / She / It / You / We / They	'll (will) play	won't (will not) play	Will … play?	Yes, … will. No, … won't.

Unit 7 Future: *Be going to*

	Affirmative	**Negative**	**Question**	**Short answers**
I	'm (am) going to play	'm not (am not) going to play	Am I going to play?	Yes, I am. No, I'm not.
He / She / It	's (is) going to play	isn't (is not) going to play	Is … going to play?	Yes, … is. No, … isn't.
You / We / They	're (are) going to play	aren't (are not) going to play	Are … going to play?	Yes, … are. No, … aren't.

Unit 8 Present perfect

	Affirmative	Negative	Question	Short answers
I / You / We / They	have discovered	haven't (have not) discovered	Have ... discovered?	Yes, ... have. No, ... haven't.
He / She / It	has discovered	hasn't (has not) discovered	Has ... discovered?	Yes, ... has. No, ... hasn't.

Unit 8 *There + to be*

	Affirmative	Negative	Question	Short answers
Present simple	There is There are	There isn't (is not) There aren't (are not)	Is there ...? Are there ...?	Yes, there is/are. No, there isn't/aren't.
Past simple	There was There were	There wasn't (was not) There weren't (were not)	Was there ...? Were there ...?	Yes, there was/were. No, there wasn't/ weren't.
Present perfect	There's been (has been) There've been (have been)	There hasn't been (has not been) There haven't been (have not been)	Has there been ...? Have there been ...?	Yes, there has/have. No, there hasn't/ haven't.
Be going to	There's (is) going to be There are going to be	There isn't (is not) going to be There aren't (are not) going to be	Is there going to be ...? Are there going to be ...?	Yes, there is/are. No, there isn't/aren't.
Future simple	There'll (will) be	There won't (will not) be	Will there be ...?	Yes, there will. No, there won't.

Irregular verbs

Infinitive	Past simple	Past participle	Infinitive	Past simple	Past participle
be	were	been	leave	left	left
beat	beat	beaten	lend	lent	lent
become	became	become	let	let	let
begin	began	begun	lie (down)	lay	lain
bend	bent	bent	light	lit	lit
bet	bet	bet	lose	lost	lost
bite	bit	bitten	make	made	made
bleed	bled	bled	mean	meant	meant
blow	blew	blown	meet	met	met
break	broke	broken	overcome	overcame	overcome
bring	brought	brought	pay	paid	paid
build	built	built	put	put	put
burn	burnt	burnt	quit	quit	quit
buy	bought	bought	read	read	read
carry	carried	carried	ride	rode	ridden
catch	caught	caught	ring	rang	rung
choose	chose	chosen	rise	rose	risen
come	came	come	run	ran	run
cost	cost	cost	say	said	said
cut	cut	cut	see	saw	seen
deal	dealt	dealt	sell	sold	sold
dig	dug	dug	send	sent	sent
dive	dived	dived	set	set	set
do	did	done	sew	sewed	sewn
draw	drew	drawn	shake	shook	shaken
drink	drank	drunk	shine	shone	shone
drive	drove	driven	show	showed	shown
dry	dried	dried	shrink	shrank	shrunk
eat	ate	eaten	shut	shut	shut
fall	fell	fallen	sing	sang	sung
feed	fed	fed	sink	sank	sunk
feel	felt	felt	sit	sat	sat
fight	fought	fought	sleep	slept	slept
find	found	found	slide	slid	slid
flee	fled	fled	speak	spoke	spoken
fly	flew	flown	spend	spent	spent
forbid	forbade	forbidden	spin	spun	spun
forget	forgot	forgotten	stand	stood	stood
forgive	forgave	forgiven	steal	stole	stolen
freeze	froze	frozen	stick	stuck	stuck
fry	fried	fried	sting	stung	stung
get	got	got	stink	stank	stunk
give	gave	given	strike	struck	struck
go	went	gone	swear	swore	sworn
grind	ground	ground	sweep	swept	swept
grow	grew	grown	swim	swam	swum
hang	hung	hung	swing	swung	swung
have	had	had	take	took	taken
hear	heard	heard	teach	taught	taught
hide	hid	hidden	tear	tore	torn
hit	hit	hit	tell	told	told
hold	held	held	think	thought	thought
hurt	hurt	hurt	throw	threw	thrown
keep	kept	kept	understand	understood	understood
kneel	knelt	knelt	wake	woke	woken
knit	knitted	knitted	wear	wore	worn
know	knew	known	weave	wove	woven
lay	laid	laid	win	won	won
lead	led	led	write	wrote	written

NOTES